The Visitation
The Divine Romance

Kathie Walters
Faith Walters

International Standard Book Number:
978-0-9629559-8-3

Published by:
Good News Fellowship Ministries
220 Sleepy Creek Rd
Macon GA 31210
(478) 757-8071   Fax (478) 757-0136
E-mail: Kathie Walters:
kathiewalters@mindspring.com
Web Site
http://www.goodnews.netministries.org

Cover Design and Typesetting
By Jerome P. Lucas
Shalom Graphics

Contents

THE VISITATION
Kathie Walters

There is a scripture in Job (chapter 10:12) that says, *"Thou hast granted me life and favor, and thy **visitation** hath preserved my Spirit."* I thank God for His visitations; they preserve and keep my Spirit according to the Word of God. I do not solely rely on experiences for my strength to walk in the Spirit, I learned and am still learning, to walk in the truth, because Jesus said, *"You shall know the truth and the truth shall make you free."* His visitations and the experiences of the supernatural realm, have always caused me to have a love-relationship with my gracious Father, His wonderful Spirit and the breathtaking Son of God - Jesus. He's the answer to every problem, the problem of every cynic and the beauty of the whole earth, for without Him, nothing was made that was made, (including the cynic, the skeptic and the atheist).

Kathie Walters

Isn't He Beautiful?

The room was beautiful, and bright,
  The reflections of the light, bounced back and forth.
    They made the gold and silver glisten,
                                and shine.

Beautiful pictures and ornaments,
  Intricate carvings, which lent delicate luxury,
    Such exquisite tapestries with colors so Divine.
        My eyes filled with wonder, at such
                              Lovely things
                              - Works of art.

Suddenly there seemed a stir among the Crowd,
  I turned to see what caused, the mellow Sound.
    I gazed with admiration on
              The most Beautiful Man,
                      I had ever seen.

His eyes were as fire, pure and bright,
His countenance like the noonday light.
His face was full of compassion, and a
Love complete.
Gentle as the dove, and wise, more than
I could ever know.

Gracious, courteous and kind,
More precious than the perfect pearl,
A man could ever find.
Majestic prince, oh love Divine. His eyes did
Shine,
With a depth of love a man
Could never Find.

He did look my way, and fixed His eyes on mine.
The love I saw there conquered me,
I gave to Him my heart.
A willing Slave to Him, who gave for me,
His all.

INTRODUCTION

THE SECRET PLACE

According to the Oxford dictionary, the definition of the word, "Secret" is *"to be kept from general knowledge, concealed, unseen, private."* Our relationship with the Lord Jesus, is first of all personal and then corporate. The corporate life of the Body of Christ only manifests itself properly and flows as the members have a real and personal relationship with God. All that we have to give comes from the Lord, via the Holy Spirit. The more I have grown in my spiritual life, the more I have realized that I do not have anything to offer in myself, that is of any eternal value, apart from the Holy Spirit.

He is the one who knows the secrets of our hearts, and He is the only one who has real knowledge and understanding of any situation. We are totally dependent upon Him. If we are left to our own thoughts and understanding, we will never have the ability to discern correctly.

In the natural realm, children are the fruit of an intimate personal relationship, so it is with spiritual fruit. The fruit that becomes evident in our lives is the result of our intimate relationship with Jesus.

He is the bridegroom, we are the betrothed, the Bride being prepared. Our first calling is to be His love, we are the apple of His eye. He has set His affection upon us. Jesus gave His life that we might have a love relationship

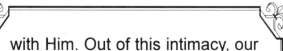

with Him. Out of this intimacy, our service and our ministries should flow and flourish. As we have sung often, *"The greatest thing in all my life is knowing You, the greatest thing in all my life is loving You, the greatest thing in all my life is serving You."* We cannot love Him unless we know Him and we cannot serve Him unless we love Him.

The Holy Spirit loves to reveal Jesus to us, and *if we seek in faith, we will surely find Him.* He promised (Matt.7:7).

I have tried to put into words a portion of two visitations I have had in the past few years.

My prayer is that you might see the Lord Jesus in a new way, or encounter something that you have not seen before, that will cause you to be even more thrilled with Jesus. Intimacy with Him can be found in the secret place, in the heart, in the center of our affection.

I have also included at the end, an account of a visitation my daughter Faith had last year when she was seventeen. It is very different from the ones that I had. The point is that young people and even small children can be visited by the Holy Spirit who loves to reveal Jesus to them. In our ministry many children have been taken up into heaven and seen and experienced a foretaste of their divine inheritance.

The Heavenly Bridegroom

Part One - May 1986

The Holy Spirit led me to spend a few days waiting on the Lord. I was not fasting particularly, nor was I striving. I was just enjoying sitting, reading my Bible and talking to the Lord. Although I was not "intense" I WAS in earnest. God does not reveal His secrets to a casual seeker. There is a place in the Holy Spirit where you can be caught up, and taken out of the realm of the natural.

This visitation was not a series of visions, (I have had many dreams and visions) but the anointing of the Lord came upon me every day for seven days. It was as real as the room I am in now. Some of this experience was very personal, and has not been included in this book, but I have included what is relevant to the Body of Christ. My desire is that you would treasure Jesus in your heart.

During the week of this first visitation, I was caught up in the Spirit every day. When everyone else had left from the house, I would spend time just waiting and thinking of the Lord. I knew that the Holy Spirit wanted to minister to me. The first morning I was sitting praying, when I saw in front of me a large rock, it was almost three feet high. It began as a vision but as I gazed at the rock, it become very real to me. It was very beautiful, and I had a deep desire and love for it. Being drawn to it, I knelt down beside it, and put my arms around it. I rested my head upon it, and I wanted to somehow become part of it. A voice spoke to me, *"This rock represents my mercy and grace, which is manifest in my Son Jesus."* When I realized why the rock was so beautiful to me, I began to weep with gratitude and joy. I had a renewed under-standing of God's great love and grace to us.

The Holy Spirit began to show me all the places in my life where I was relying on something else for my acceptance with the Father. He kept revealing things to me, and I wept until I felt that I was in small pieces. Then I threw myself upon the rock totally, and repented of trusting in all the GOOD THINGS, instead of His grace ALONE. Prayer and Bible reading, giving, good works, witnessing are all commendable and valuable things, but they are not a substitute for His grace. They cannot add to our salvation.

God is very jealous, He does not want us to put our trust in anything or anyone else. When I was through weeping and repenting, the voice spoke to me again. *"The rock has now become your shield and hiding place, your high tower, your rock, your light and your fortress and defense."* I had been saved for twenty five years at that point. It is easy to fall back into a works mentality.

The visitation continued that

night in a dream. In the dream I was in a great palace; it was very beautiful.

In Europe, there are many palaces, some of you have enjoyed visiting them. There are parts of the palace that are open to the public, in order that the people may have access to see all the treasures. In many instances the Prince or Duke may still live in the Palace. The stairways that lead to His private rooms are roped and sectioned off. Such was this palace that I found myself. I began walking through a vast hall, amongst crowds of people. They were all gazing in awe at the wonderful treasures that belonged to the Prince. The ornaments, paintings and breathtaking furnishings - each item was a wonder in itself. Great carved ceil-

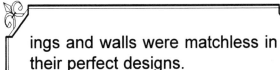

ings and walls were matchless in their perfect designs.

I suddenly noticed the Prince, who owned the palace. He began to walk among the crowds. I could not take my eyes from Him and all the other lovely things around me faded in comparison. He was so BEAUTIFUL! Something about His loveliness took my breath away. I fell in love with Him totally, and as I gazed at Him, His countenance shone. He was full of grace and compassion. He was courteous and kind, gentle and loving, yet strong. His personality was made up of purity and truth. I saw him pause and talk to someone here and there, never irritable or angry, always gracious and kind. Even in His correction, He was so gracious. I was amazed. I knew instinctively He loved me deeply. It was hard to believe. I could see His eyes as they met mine. I had never seen such love expressed in a glance.

The people who were milling around, looking at the treasures, sometimes turned and looked at the Prince. Many of them smiled, but they turned again and continued looking at the treasures around them. I felt sad, because He was SO WONDERFUL AND SO VERY BEAUTIFUL. I COULDN'T UNDERSTAND why they would want to look at anything else. It is so easy to get our attention on the wonderful gifts that God has given us, or the great revelations, visions and supernatural things. He has given us so many blessings to enjoy because He loves us so much. It is a pity that so many times we get our attention on the blessings, spend time enjoying those blessings and forgetting the source of every good gift. Even our ministries sometimes take all our time and attention, and we forget who we are ministering with.

The Prince began to talk to a group of people and I felt a jealousy rise up in my heart, as His attention was taken from me. These people were infringing upon my fellowship with Him. Afterward He turned to me and explained that He cared for them also. He spoke with such tenderness and love that my feeling of jealousy melted and I felt ashamed of my selfishness. I was awakened by one of my children who had a need.

I returned to sleep about 2am

when the dream continued. This time though I found myself in a banqueting hall. It was in the upper part of the palace. I was allowed to come and go to His private chambers. I found myself seated at a long, beautiful banqueting table. Opposite me, also seated, was a man that I knew from our Bible Study group. The man was trying to explain a revelation He had received, but he was not too good at putting it together. I got impatient and interrupted. The Prince put His finger to His lips and just looked at me. His eyes spoke, *"Be patient, this man loves me."* Again I felt so ashamed. My attitude was awful, especially in the light of one so kind and gracious. After awaking, I cried for an hour.

The following morning I became overawed by the goodness of the Lord. The dream had left a deep impression on my heart. I had such a wonderful revelation of the Lord Jesus. I did not realize until later, that this experience was going to continue for six more days.

A few hours later a friend came to my home to pray with me. As I told her about the dream, I began to weep again as I remembered the people who had become more interested in the treasures than the Prince who owned them. As I continued speaking, the Holy Spirit began to lift me again out of the natural realm. This time I found myself seated in a chair, near a large majestic fireplace. I was waiting for the Prince to come and speak to me. Slowly He walked toward me, He was so incredibly lovely. He was

perfect in every way, and such love!
I was again breathless in His presence. He sat and took my hand.
Then He allowed me to ask some
questions.

Let me first explain this part . . . in
the downstairs part of the palace,
where the general public gathered,
was a large beautiful staircase. The
stairs being covered in deep red
carpet, it had the appearance of
velvet. At each side of the first step
was a footman (an angel). There
was a silk rope stretched across the
entrance of the stairs. It acted as a
barrier, so that the people could not
have access to the upper part of the
palace. I asked Him why that barrier was there, preventing people
coming to the private rooms. The
Prince told me that anyone could, if
they wanted to see HIM and the
angels would remove the rope

instantly.. He explained that there were many people whose *ONLY INTEREST WAS, IN SEEING MORE TREASURES.* The treasures in the upper part of the palace were more personal and precious than those in the large courtroom downstairs.

The second question I asked was, *"Don't you mind that many of the people hardly notice you? They acknowledge who you are, but they turn away to look at all your treasures."* He replied, *"It will not always be like this."* He showed me a vision of Himself. In the vision He was standing at the top of the great stairway and there were many people standing below. He looked very majestic, He had on royal robes. Every eye turned to Him, and it became very silent. Each person bowed and knelt before Him.

He said that one day soon, ALL of His people would allow Him to truly rule and reign in their lives and as they did, His life would flow through His Body as it should. He explained that in that day the Body of Christ will come into the authority that He ordained for us. I asked another question, *"Will you take care of us?"* It was a strange question to me, as the Lord had always taken care of us wonderfully. *"No good thing will I withhold from You,"* He smiled as He answered. I proceeded, *"Can I have a fresh anointing and new baptism in the Spirit?"* He questioned me as to why I wanted it. I had to stop and think. The question I asked did not come from my intellect, but from somewhere deep inside. *"I want to go and tell the people in the great hall how wonderful you are. If I don't have a real anointing from your Spirit, they will not listen to me."* It must have been an acceptable answer because He said that I would, *"Have it as I went." "What about David?"* (My husband) was my next question. At that moment David entered the room. He came and knelt beside the Prince. The Prince put his hand upon David's shoulder. Neither spoke. It was as though both knew what was in each other's heart, and it was not necessary to talk. I spoke up, *"Shall we go now and speak to the people?" "Go"*, He replied.

When we reached the door, a footman (angel) appeared and put a long red robe upon David's shoulders. Outside the door, I stopped to tell another footmen how wonderful the Prince was. He seemed pleased that I told him, but he already knew. He smiled at me.

When we reached the bottom of the stairs, I told another footmen how marvelous the Prince was, but he knew also. He was happy for me at my great discovery!

As I mingled with the crowd of people downstairs, I told them about the wonderful Prince. I spoke of His loving-kindness. His grace and mercy, His longsuffering and holiness, His tenderness and purity. They listened to me and I was very happy. Each time I met with the Prince it left me crying for a long time. He was exceedingly lovely.

The following Sunday another friend, Glendon, came to pray with me, but the Prince spoke to me to come and spend time with Him first. I went into another room and waited. I felt the anointing come and again I was lifted up into the Spirit.

The Prince came and stood before me. I was unable to speak. He leaned toward me and put a yoke around my neck, and shoulders. It startled me. I asked Him what the yoke was. He said that it represented responsibility. He continued, "If you go in My Name then you must be responsible with My power." I felt a little scared because I knew how easy it was for me to get into the flesh. Although the yoke was not heavy, I was conscious of it. The Prince smiled gently, He was very understanding. I then walked through the door toward the great staircase and as I did another footman met me. He placed flowers of different colors on top of the yoke. *"The reason,"* He said, *"Was so that other people would not see the yoke. They would only see the flowers"* (blessings).

The following three days, the Holy Spirit came strongly upon me and took me into the presence of the Lord. It was a very personal, Song of Solomon, experience. Jesus reached into the depths of my being and I cannot describe what happened. My heart was broken, not with grief, but with wonder and awe.

A human vessel cannot fully comprehend the love of God toward us. We can only take just a little experience of it. During that time, Jesus took me to His Father. Afterward, Jesus put His arms around me and my heart began to become one with His heart, like a vine intertwining. I was full of joy and thankfulness.

The final day He sent for me again. I wondered what else there could be. I waited. This time I found myself walking along the balcony toward the staircase with David.

The Prince was walking between us. His appearance was very regal. He said, *"I will go with you."* This was the end of this visitation. I pray that my attention never again wanders from Jesus.

He is THE ONE who is to reign in His church. Our eyes must be for Him. His grace and mercy ALONE are responsible for everything we are and have. We are complete in Him. He will not share His glory with any man. If He does all the work, then He gets all the glory. We have not contributed anything to our redemption. Our part is just to yield to Him. The yielding comes in our relationship, in the secret place.

The Holy Spirit is always willing to reveal the loveliness of Jesus to us, if we take the time to look for Him. He will draw you, but you must go after Him. He is my beloved and He is my friend. He is altogether lovely (Song of Sol. 5:16). Respond to His invitation. *"Rise my love, my fair one, and come away, the winter is past, the rain is over and gone, the time of singing has come"* (Song of Sol. 2:10).

THE BRIDE
Part Two

(1 Peter 3:15). "Sanctify," according to my Oxford Dictionary, means, *"To set apart as holy, keep pure."* To sanctify the Lord in our heart means to have that place set apart for the Lord. To be kept for Him, He is our holiness. For many years as a good evangelical Christian, I struggled to be holy, but I failed miserably. When I was filled with the HOLY Spirit I decided to receive His holiness instead. In twelve years as a Christian I hadn't found one ounce of my own. When Jesus gave us his life, it was holy and sanctified. The word of God says, *"If we walk in the Spirit **WE WILL NOT** fulfill the lusts of the flesh"* (Gal. 5:16). I spent all my effort trying not to fulfill the lusts of the flesh, in order to qualify to walk in the Spirit. I had it the wrong

way around and had to learn by faith to walk in the Spirit. Then I found that *I DID NOT* fulfill the lusts of the flesh. The life of the Spirit was so exciting and Jesus was so real that I wasn't interested in the flesh. Besides, it didn't have anything of value to offer. The flesh is simply like a rotten landlord, he wants the rent, but doesn't care about doing anything for the tenant.

In Romans, chapter six it says that we were *crucified with Christ*. We are free from that old (flesh) Landlord, we don't owe him anything. We don't have to obey his voice or his leading. It is a great release and relief when this revelation comes. He sets us FREE from striving and gives us peace. Salvation from beginning to end is ALL of Him, not some of Him and some of our own effort. It is not even most of Him and a little of us. IT'S ALL OF HIM. A dear friend of mine often quotes this when he is preaching.

> *"God can do a little*
> *with a lot,*
> *A lot with a little,*
> *But everything with nothing."*

If we could just get a handle on that, it would save us from so much struggling. The Lord Jesus is responsible. He is the one who is going to, *"Present us faultless before the presence of His Father with exceeding joy"* (Jude 24). Do you know that Jesus will not give up that right to another. He will not allow anyone else to present you faultless before The Father. It's His prerogative, for you are His treasure, His love. He has set His affection upon you and you are the apple of His eye. Your pastor, your friend, even your husband or wife, cannot present you faultless to The Father in this way, for they have the same need of a mediator as you do.

When there is no condemnation, we are free to enjoy the love of Jesus. When we enjoy that communion and sweetness that comes from our relationship with the Great Shepherd, then we can develop an intimate relationship in that secret place. The Song of Solomon is not a fairy tale, but a love story.

SECOND
VISITATION
SPRING 1992

A well known prophetic friend of mine, Bob Jones, was talking to me on the telephone. I mentioned the visitation I had in May 86. He said casually, *"I think you are about to have another one."* I didn't give it too much thought that day, but the next morning an angel was standing in my kitchen, He spoke to me about a couple of things, and I thought that this must be the visitation Bob spoke of. I did not dream of what was to happen next.

The Holy Spirit began to come upon me in an unusual way. It was similar to the visitation I had previously, except this time most of the anointings came when I was driving. I was living in a small town about 40 minutes from Charlottesville, Virginia. The help we had in our office at that time was mostly from friends, who came during the evenings to take care of our book orders and such. Most days I would go to the main post office in Charlottesville to mail them out and take care of other office necessities.

I thoroughly enjoyed those beautiful daily drives amid the lanes and trees and flowers. I would pray and worship the Lord all the way to town and home again. There were some old praise tapes that I had forgotten about, so I began to play them on my car stereo.

One day while driving, I was caught up By the Holy Spirit and taken into the Heavenlies.

The first day I remember standing and watching the Lord Jesus. He was carrying in His arms a young girl, in the way you would carry a heavier child. Her arms were around His neck and her legs were around His waist. Her features were perfect, as if they were sculptured. But, her face gave an impression of hardness. She looked about 12 years old. His arm was under her, holding her up. She was carrying a toy in her right hand. I remember thinking to myself, *"At least she has the sense to hold on to Him, that's all she has got going for her."* I must have watched for a long time because I found myself at my destination. I thought it was interesting, but felt it was a pity that the young woman, who represented the betrothed, looked so immature and selfish.

This same theme unfolded before my eyes every day when I drove to Charlottesville.

I had no idea of how I finally arrived at my destination each day, I just somehow managed to end up where I should be. I had little recollection of the actual drive. I began to watch a story unfold, a beautiful love story. I cannot remember all the instances that occurred day after day, but I saw the young girl grow up into a very lovely young lady. She was dependent upon Jesus and so she had to stay with Him. She observed how marvelous He was. She saw His kindness and graciousness; His perfection. Everything He did emanated deep love. He was holy, but not religious, as some of us think of as holy. He was without fault. She never wanted to leave His side.

A strange thing happened. Because she was constantly with Him, she fell deeply in love with Him. Do you know what else? She became just like Him. She began to manifest the same grace and love and kindness as Jesus. She became the same as He was. She didn't try or strive to do it, it just HAPPENED. In 2 Cor 3:17,18, it says, *"Where the Spirit of the Lord is, there is liberty. But we all with open face (without guilt) beholding as in a glass the glory of the Lord, are changed into the same image from glory to glory, even as by the spirit of the Lord."*

Willard Jarvis, a pastor and good friend of ours from Columbus, Ohio, once said in a sermon, *"WHAT GETS YOUR ATTENTION, GETS YOU."* It's true! We become just like what we are looking at. If all your attention is given to something, you will get caught up in it and it will manifest itself in your life. If you get your attention on your problems you will never get free. If you put all your attention on Jesus and love Him, you will become just like Him. You will not have to struggle and strive to be spiritual. You will be naturally spiritual.

A duck does not have to struggle to learn how to swim, it has been created for the water. So are you created for the realm of the spirit when you are born again. We learn to guard the secret place of the heart and yield to the Spirit of God. His power is manifested in our yielding, and not in our striving.

One day when I was in the Spirit, I saw the young woman standing in a room, there were three angels standing there also. Jesus came into the room and His presence brought such joy that the angels began to shout and leap. I felt ashamed! I had been in many meetings and the joy of the Lord had come and I couldn't be bothered to make the effort to dance or even get up out of my seat. He deserves that we praise Him with ALL our being, with all our hearts.

Several days later, I was driving and worshipping; Singing with a very anointed tape, from Grace Fellowship in Oklahoma. They were singing, *"Isn't He beautiful, beautiful, isn't He."* Now the way this church sings the song is a little different from some. In the middle, the words change and they sing, *"Yes you are, beautiful, beautiful, yes you are."* I was caught up into a very light place, again, there were three angels standing nearby. As Jesus walked toward us, they turned toward the young women and began to sing to her. They were singing the words with the tape. They opened their hands toward the Lord. *"Isn't He beautiful, beautiful isn't He? Counselor, Almighty God, isn't He?"*

They continued to sing and the young woman joined in, worshipping and agreeing with the angels. Suddenly, the Lord Jesus turned to her and took her hand in His, He looked deep into her eyes and sang *"Yes you are, beautiful, beautiful yes you are."* I could see such exquisite love and devotion when He looked at her. I thought, *"He totally adores His betrothed."* I could never describe His countenance. There are no words that I know. Such love! It was so awesome and pure that I could not contain it. It was too much for me. I found myself back in the car, the presence of God so strong I pulled off the highway to the side of the road, devastated, but not in a negative way. I felt I was in a thousand little pieces. I wept and wept, as this love immersed me.

As I saw the look of love and grace upon the face of the Lord Jesus, I was never able to see the Body of Christ in quite the same way again. Sometimes when I am praying for people, especially the women at some of the women's meetings that I minister in, I see the stress and anxiety on the faces of my sisters in the Lord and I say to them, *"If only you could catch a glimpse of His face. He looks at you with such love and compassion."*

He is devoted to us. He gave His all that we might be made His cherished possession. He extended great grace to each of us. We do not have the right to withhold that same grace from another, for He said, *"Freely you have received, freely give."* I do believe that if we withhold grace from another, then God will withhold that grace from us in one area or another. For if we eliminate the grace which we have received, then we make a transfer into judgement. *"The same judgement that we mete (give out to others) will be meted (given out) to us again."(Matt.7:2).*

Day after day the visitation continued. Another time I saw the young women come and kneel at His feet, she acknowledged Him as Lord of Lords. The Lord Jesus gave her a chalice, a golden censor. He stood and pointed, He told her to go to every nation and gather the great harvest, gather the prayers of all the saints being offered before the throne (See Revelation 8:3).

There were so many things that the Holy Spirit revealed. I saw the great wedding feast. It was truly glorious, the most wonderful, incredible experience. There are no words invented to describe the glories of the Kingdom of Heaven. I saw Jesus invite His Bride to share His throne. The Holy Spirit showed me people from every tribe, kindred and nation come to the heavenly Mount Zion, singing, with everlasting joy upon their heads.

The visitation I had this time lasted three and a half weeks. I believe there is a significance in that. My attempt to portray some revelations of the Spirit, is feeble I know. My desire is to encourage you to believe. The Holy Spirit desires to make real to you our great and precious inheritance - the great promises, for by these we are partakers of the divine nature (2 Pet 1:4).

Beloved, our inheritance is not

religious information, that we may have head knowledge about the Bible, or even about God. Our inheritance is God's beloved Son, Jesus, and His Kingdom. Religious spirits don't mind if we know lots of scriptures; The devil does not want us to fall in love with the heavenly Bridegroom. Jesus is the Lily of the Valley, the Bright and Morning Star, the Fairest of Ten Thousand. The glory of the Lord will be upon our faces, but His face will outshine them all. Let the light of His countenance shine on you.

AN AWESOME GOD
Faith Walters,
July 1994

At the last minute I had an opportunity to go to some revival meetings in Kentucky. I jumped at the chance to go to the meetings being held by Rodney Howard Brown.

The meetings lasted all week. Many people were being touched with a spirit of laughter and I had a wonderful time worshipping the Lord. I prayed constantly that God would touch me also. One night a couple sang a song, *"We are standing on holy ground,"* and I had a vision of Jesus coming down with His arms outstretched. As He did, a cloud of glory spread over the people. The last night I asked the Lord again to touch me. I wept on and off for two hours.

I had a very intense desire in my heart that brought me to tears. The following day we headed back to Atlanta and I felt a little disappointed because I wanted to be drunk in the Holy Spirit. The Lord told me that it wasn't time. My friend, Jessica was very drunk.

When we arrived back at Jessica's home, where I was to spend the night, we spent more time praying and waiting on the Lord. Suddenly everyone got drunk in the Spirit at the same time. (My friend and I, three adults and four younger children). One three year old boy got a strong anointing and began to blow on everyone. Everyone fell out in the Spirit. For a while, we could only speak in tongues to one another.

During this time I had a vision of

myself. I was running through a jungle with natives all around me. Then I saw tens of thousands of African people gathered together praising the Lord. Then I saw myself, building something with my hands. Each one of us was touched in some special way. My feet began to burn. Then another lady, her little girl and I, ran around the house praising God.

The anointing stayed upon the children and teens all evening until we went to bed. Jessica and I slept in her living room as there were so many people in the house. About 11:30pm a young boy, Josh, who was staying also in the house, came out of his room into the living room, where Jessica and I were trying to sleep. He was shaking and said, *"I saw an angel."* We asked him about it and he explained further, *"The angel had a white robe with gold trim and he was blowing a golden trumpet, there were two other angels standing with him, with their hands raised."* We prayed, the Lord gave me the word, *"Jubilee."*

We asked Jesus to reveal Himself to us, as we desired to see Him with our natural eyes. Suddenly, Josh and I began to shake. We became terrified - not scared - but terrified. Josh said that he felt the presence of the Lord and that Jesus was there. We then began to shake violently. I had never felt like that in my whole life.

Jesus began to reveal Himself to us, but not as the gentle, loving Jesus that we wanted to see. What we began to see was the Jesus of Revelation chapter one. The Jesus that John saw on the Isle of

Patmos, with hair like wool and eyes like fire and a two edged sword in His mouth. We could not look upon Him, but we knew He was there and we could feel His Presence. I felt that If I looked up and saw Him, I would not be able to live through it. We then began to pray, *"Oh Lord, please do not reveal yourself to us, we are not worthy to behold you."* All three of us began to weep as we cried this prayer out to God. We asked Him to prepare our hearts so that one day we may look upon Him. Then our cries turned into worship and we told Him how beautiful He was and how much we loved Him.

When we looked up again, we saw a silver mist a short distance from us. For a moment, it took the shape of a man. We just looked and worshiped God. We got up from the floor, trembling. We moved toward the mist. Before we reached it, Josh and I fell to our knees. Jessica went down with her face on the floor. We stayed there worshipping and praying, then it lifted. We were too overwhelmed to say anything and so we just went back to bed.

The following morning at Jessica's church, the Holy Spirit told me a number of things.

First, He told me, "Not to be quick to be ready. You cannot make yourself ready by your own actions." He said, "To be ready, I have to NOT BE READY, so that HE can make me ready.

Second, He told me that my ministry would carry praise to the nations and the nations would run with Jubilee.

Third, He said that I was to be

greedy for Him, but not selfish. Then the Lord began to speak more and I wrote it down (as if the Lord was speaking):

"I WANT TO ANOINT YOU FOR THE NATIONS. I WANT TO USE YOU LIKE I'VE NEVER USED YOU BEFORE. YIELD TO ME. WORSHIP ME. YOU WILL DO MANY WORKS IN MANY NATIONS. YOU WILL BE INVOLVED, YOU WILL BE BLESSED. MANY CHILDREN SHALL CALL YOU BY NAME. THEY SHALL INHERIT MY KINGDOM. THEY SHALL BE THE LAST GENERATION TO BE CHALLENGED. THEY WILL GO OUT AND CALL ME 'LORD.' THEY SHALL SEE VISIONS AND RIDE IN CHARIOTS. THEY SHALL WALK ON THE WATER AND HEAL THE SICK. THIS WILL BE THEIR DAILY LIVES. THIS WILL BE NORMAL. MY SPIRIT WILL BE

POURED OUT SO STRONG, PEOPLE THAT RESIST ME WILL BE STRUCK DEAD. THESE DAYS ARE SERIOUS. THESE DAYS ARE COMING TO AN END, MY JUDGMENT WILL BE COMING SOON - IT'S ON ITS WAY. IF THE PEOPLE ARE NOT BLESSED, THEN THEY ARE CONDEMNED. MY MERCY WILL ONLY BE FOR THOSE WHO SEEK ME. THOSE WHO DON'T, WILL BE DESTROYED. THEY SHALL CEASE TO WALK, TO LIVE, TO BE. EVERYONE WILL KNOW THAT I AM GOD."

I am still filled, but I have to learn to walk in it. I pray this experience stays with me always. It is so exciting and challenging: It is the only way to live. God can use anyone. He proved that when He used three year old Nathan, in such a powerful way. God can show you things in the supernatural and use you mightily for His glory. All we have to do is submit ourselves to

Him and believe Him.

It is the most awesome adventure to be a Christian who is fired up and in tune with God. A dead Christian is no Christian at all. God is moving on the young people today, He is calling them, anointing them and using them. My sister, Lisa has been in so many nations, witnessing and preaching the gospel. She just returned from China, where she led a team of young people, two of whom were only twelve years old. She is waiting for her next mission adventure. She is only fifteen years old.

Don't be one who misses out on what God is doing in these days. Give yourself to Him and your life will never be the same.

Faith Walters

Books by David Walters

Kids in Combat - Handbook for Youth Pastors, Parents and Teachers.

Equipping the Younger Saints - Teaching children spiritual gifts.

Children Aflame - Accounts of the Holy Spirit moving upon young children during the John Wesley revivals and the ministry of David Walters.

The Anointing and You -   (How to Understand Revival) What we must do to receive, sustain, impart, and channel the outpouring and pass it on to the younger generation.

Worship fur Dummies - David Walters calls himself a dummy in the area of praise and worship, but he knows the ways of the Holy Spirit.

Radical Living in a Godless Society
Our godless Society really targets our children and youth. How do we cope with this situation?

Illustrated Bible Studies
for young people.

Armor of God - A children's Bible study on Ephesians 6:10-18. Illustrated (for ages 6-15 years)

Fact or Fantasy - A children's study book on Christian Apologetics (for ages 6-15 years).

Being a Christian - A children's scripture study book. How to make sure you are really born again. (for ages 6-15 years).

Fruit of the Spirit - A children's scripture study on the Fruit of the Spirit.(ages 7-15 years).

Children's Prayer Manual - Children's study on prayer (ages 8-14 years).

The Gifts of the Spirit- Children's Bible study on the Gifts of the Spirit (ages 7-adults).

Books by Kathie Walters

Living in the Supernatural - Learn to live in the Supernatural realm, and get to know the ways of the Holy Spirit.

Angels Watching over You - Did you know that Angels are very active in our everyday lives?

Celtic Flames -Discover the exciting accounts of famous Fourth & Fifth Century Celtic Christians: Patrick, Brendan, Cuthbert, Brigid and others.

Columba - The Celtic Dove - Read about the prophetic and miraculous ministry of this famous Celtic Christian, filled with supernatural visitations.

Parenting - By The Spirit - How to discipline your children by the Spirit and enable them to fulfill God's destiny call on their lives.

The Spirit of False Judgment - How to know when you are operating in the Spirit of False Judgment instead of understanding knowing God's heart.

Elitism & the False Shepherding Spirit This book discusses Control, Manipulation, False Shepherding Spirit, Spirit of Abortion, Grief and how to be set free from them.

The Bright and Shining Revival - An account of the Hebrides Revival 1948 - 1952

Please write or call
for current pricing:

GOOD NEWS MINISTRIES
220 Sleepy Creek Rd.
Macon GA 31210
(478)757-8071 Fax:(478)757-0136
E-mail: Kathie Walters
kathiewalters@mindspring.com
Web Site
http://www.goodnews.netministries.org

ABOUT THE WALTERS FAMILY

DAVID AND KATHIE WALTERS are originally from England. They have lived and ministered in the United States for eighteen years. They presently reside in Macon, Georgia.

DAVID has a burden for what he terms church-wise kids & teens. Those who have been brought up in the church and have a head knowledge of the things of God. His desire is for the young people to have a dynamic experience of God for themselves. His "Raising Anointed Children and Youth." seminars are for children/teens, youth pastors and parents - He also holds revival meetings for churches and includes the children and teens in the miracle ministry of the Holy Spirit. David ministers at many National Conferences in the U.S. and overseas.

KATHIE ministers alongside David and also has a desire to see God's women come forth in all their anointings and giftings. She believes that the realm of the Spirit, the supernatural power of God, heaven and angels are our inheritance and are meant to be a normal part of our lives and the life of the church. She also believes in Spirit-Led Parenting.

FAITH, 17, and LISA, 14, are anointed and already moving in their giftings. They both love to travel. Faith ministers in dance and prophecy and Lisa sings and ministers the gifts of the Spirit.